Coin Collecting User Guide

A complete manual for dummies, beginners and seniors on how to start coin collection and easily make fun and money from your hobby.

August T. Wrights

Copyright © 2021

All rights reserved, no part of this publication shall be reproduced, stored in a retrieval system, or transmitted via any means be it electronic, mechanical, photocopying, recording, or otherwise, without written permission from the publisher. Although every precaution has been taken in the preparation of this book, the publisher and author assume no responsibility for errors or omissions. Nor is any liability assumed for damages resulting from the use of the information contained herein.

CHAPTER ONE 1
   Introduction to Coin Collecting....................................... 1
   What makes a rare coin expensive? 5
   When were the first coins used?...................................... 6
   Is the metal in the coins valuable? 6
   Why is coin collection so common? 7
   How are new pieces created? 8
CHAPTER TWO 10
   What to gather for rare coin valuation?........................... 10
   What factors contribute to the value of a rare coin? 12
   How to keep your coins in good condition 14
CHAPTER THREE 15
   What is numismatics?... 15
   What are coin varieties 15
   Coins of Greece and Rome.. 16
   Coins of Islam 18
   Coins of British 19
   Coins of the universal... 22
   Coins of Continental Europe 24
   Coins of Russia and China 25
CHAPTER FOUR.. 26
   How to properly invest in valuable coins?..................... 26
   How are coins made? 28
   Raw Materials from Mining.. 28
   Tossing 30

Blanking 31
Polishing 32
Cleaning and annealing 33
Distressing 34
Striking or stamping 35
Distribution 36

CHAPTER FIVE 37
Where can to sell valuable coins? 37
Sell to a Coin Shop 37
Physical Auction 38
Online Auction or Marketplace 38
How to give value to your coin? 39
Consider a Valuation 39
Get a feel for your worth 40
How to get your coin ready for sale 41
How to examine the coin holder 41
Consider getting a CAC sticker 42
How to select the appropriate time to sell coins 43
How to determine if a collection should be grouped or divided? 44

CHAPTER SIX 45
How to understand the Four Coin Values 45
Special notes on coin variations 46
Coins from the American colonies 47
Gold Coins from the Pioneer Territorial and Early Branch Mints 48

Coinage with a Pattern 49
Coins of Today (Including Proofs) 50
How to recognize a fake coin 52
Follow your intuition 52
Determine the size and weight 53
Pay attention to the intricacies 54

CHAPTER SEVEN 55
How to keep track of your coins? 55
Simple ways to catalog your coins 57
Documentation 58
Checklist for Purchasing 59
Spreadsheet 59
Software 61
How to sort coins 62
How to use the Coin Grading Scale of 70 Points? 63

CHAPTER EIGHT 68
How to use the Three Grade Buckets for Sorting Coins? 68
What is the best way to grade Circulated Coins? 70
Step one 70
Step two 71
Step three 71
Pictorial Coinage of The United States 72

CHAPTER ONE

Introduction to Coin Collecting

For thousands of years, humans have been drawn to collecting. Collecting, whether of rocks, shells, books, tools, or coins, arouses curiosity and interest in all of us. Collecting causes time to stop and brings the past with us. We would not know the past if nothing was saved.

Coins are a traditional collectible item. The possibility to hold a piece of history used by people in the past has made coin collecting a popular hobby loved by people of all ages. Coins are also becoming more popular as a form of investment.

The value of collectible coins is determined by two primary factors: scarcity and condition. Collectors and dealers determine prices depending on demand. This is mostly accomplished through auctions and a network of coin dealers. Coins might be appealing owing to their cultural or historical importance in addition to their rarity and condition. Due to their international popularity, coins depicting notable historical individuals frequently command a premium.

Collectible coins are distinct from bullion coins, the worth of which is determined entirely by the weight of the precious metal contained within them. Scarcity, the most valuable collectible coins are available in extremely restricted quantities. If you own a rare object in excellent condition, you may expect its value to rise in the future. The value of a rare coin is determined and evolves as a result of broad collector or investment demand. Although hoards of coins are periodically discovered, supply is typically rigidly confined to recognized market pieces.

A market that is honest and transparent A dealer network is used to buy and sell coins. Some focus on certain areas of the coin market. Coins are also purchased and sold during coin shows and auctions.

It is a worldwide market that is not dominated by a single player. Prices are determined by supply and demand. Auction records serve as a reference point for prices and values, and virtually every form of the coin has well-documented historical price patterns.

Collectibles bring the past to life. It is remembered through artifacts used by those who lived before us. This is especially true with coins, which were (and still are) the medium of daily business. When you touch a coin that is 50, 200, or 2,000 years old in your palm, you can't help but wonder where it has been in its lifetime! Coins serve as historical relics. You are holding a piece of history in your hands, whether it is an antique coin or a more modern coin commemorating important individuals or events.

What makes a rare coin expensive?

A coin's value is not determined only by its age. For example, some 1,600year-old Roman coins may still be acquired today for $20 or less! The value of a coin, like the value of most other commodities, is determined by supply and demand. Demand is a big issue. Some coin denominations, such as Buffalo nickels or Mercury dimes, are more popular than others. As a result of more collectors vying for the same coins, their values will rise. The value of a coin is governed by the interconnected elements of scarcity, condition, and demand.

Perhaps more coins of an earlier date were made than those of a later date, thus coins from a far earlier period may still be accessible. This is called supply. Of course, it all depends on how many of each have been rescued and in what state. The condition of a coin (the state in which it has been maintained) is an enormously essential element in its worth. An uncirculated coin may be valued tens of thousands of times more than a circulating coin of the same period.

When were the first coins used?

Though the earliest coins are credited to Lydia in Asia Minor about 600-700 B.C., it is now thought that copper coins were used in China hundreds of years earlier.

However, because the Lydians were likely unaware of China's existence, their coins – known as "Staters" (a unit of weight) – were created separately. The original Staters were fashioned of electrum, a natural gold-silver alloy.

Is the metal in the coins valuable?

Gold and silver coins have two values: numismatic (collector) value and intrinsic (precious metal) worth. Bigger quality coins will command a higher premium above their metal value than lower grade or condition coins.

Why is coin collection so common?

Coin collecting is an interesting pastime since money is something that people use now that was utilized in the past. Coins, which have mostly been produced by official governments, might remember thrilling moments in American and world history. You receive a sense of satisfaction and pride no matter how much time you spend on a collection.

After a hard day, you may unwind by going through it coin by coin. Your coins will almost certainly survive you by hundreds or thousands of years! Take good care of them, and future collectors will appreciate your consideration.

How are new pieces created?

Hammered coins were handcrafted by striking two dies with a hammer. The dies had the imprint for either side of the coin on the interior. Often, the monarch's or emperor's head was on one side. The coin's denomination and other designs were on the reverse side. These coins' themes, particularly those from the Greek and Roman worlds, may be nothing short of magnificent. Master artisans, including sculptors, were frequently hired to engrave dies for Greek towns, resulting in beautiful miniature masterpieces. The hammer-striking technique was not precise, and coins from the ancient and medieval cultures can be somewhat off-center. This gives individuality to the century-old coins while also ensuring that no two coins are precisely similar.

Milled coins first appeared approximately 400 years ago. They were mass-produced beginning in the mid-seventeenth century and are machine-made. They have considerably better definition and consistency. Coin machining also allowed for the inclusion of serrated edges and inscriptions, which aided in the prevention of fraud and clipping. Mechanized manufacturing also coincided with advances in realism and style brought forth by the Renaissance two centuries before. For the first time, European kings appeared in stunning realism on their coins. We'll discuss the condition of the coins you purchase afterward. This is a whole other topic. The condition of the coin is critical to its worth.

CHAPTER TWO

What to gather for rare coin valuation?

Coin collectors often seek to amass a collection of coins from a single nation or set of countries. They could be looking for coins from a specific historical period. Others seek after coins with special features. These might be commemorative sets or sets with faults, for example. Many collections are built around coins that seem similar yet have slightly different die designs. Tokens, which are used as a substitute for tiny change in various nations at particular periods, are also a popular collectible.

A frequent collecting theme is a set series, which includes one coin of each kind and value for each year the coin was produced during that ruler's reign. This might also incorporate any design modifications that have been implemented. It might include coins produced by various mints. There are several subtleties.

In the first place, it makes sense to collect and invest in coins from the nation where you reside or from a historical period in which you have a particular interest. You will most likely be more aware of its history and better able to assess what makes a specific coin unique.

From a practical viewpoint, it makes sense for UK collectors and investors to buy British coins, and for US collectors and investors to acquire American coins. The home market will have the highest amount of coin trading and the greatest number of collectors, dealers, and investors in this sort of coin. The Ancient Coin market, on the other hand, is steady and worldwide, having collectors in almost every country.

Some coins are undeniably uncommon. There are several examples of coins where only a few copies were made and then the design was discontinued. Proofs and mistakes – coins created to test a new pattern or those where a slight manufacturing fault resulted in an uncommon version of a popular coin are also a good hunting field for individuals looking for something rare for financial purposes.

What factors contribute to the value of a rare coin?

A collectible coin's value is determined by factors other than supply and demand, such as its date and design, mintmarks, and condition. The condition of the coin is the most crucial of these. One of the responsibilities of an expert you could work with is to be able to correctly evaluate the condition of a coin. A numismatist can also advise you on how to maintain the coin in that condition after you've purchased it.

The condition of an item is critical to its worth. So, how do you solve it? The four major differences in grade for an antique coin are shown below. Third-party firms may grade medieval and contemporary coins using numerical increments of condition.

The vocabulary used to describe a coin's grading is subjective, and some dealers are more careful than others in the grade they assign. This speaks in favor of dealing with a renowned and long-established merchant, such as A. H. Baldwin & Sons Ltd, whose grades are constant and trustworthy. Less reputable sellers may overvalue coins.

A coin's tone is also significant. A toned coin has developed a color that is deeper and richer than the original. It is most often used in ancient coins. When it comes to ancient coins, an appealing natural tone may make a piece more valued.

Most collectors like contemporary coins to keep their full luster as if they were recently struck. A brown or green patina on ancient bronze and copper coins, on the other hand, may considerably boost their value due to greater visual appeal.

The tone is also seen in ancient coins composed of precious metals. Silver may have a golden tone up to nearly black or plum color. Tone can also influence the elevated areas of the coin differently from the rest of the coin. The beauty of the tone might be subjective to some extent. However, a beautifully toned coin may (and frequently does) command a significant premium.

The legend (text around the coin) might affect its worth, especially if the monarch's name has been misspelled or shortened. This is typical on earlier coins where the literacy of people who made the coins was low. Another distinctive characteristic is the mintmark on the coin, which is generally a single letter indicating where it was produced. They, too, have the potential to have a major impact on value.

How to keep your coins in good condition

Protecting your collection is a topic in and of itself. Valuable coins should be insured and safely stored in a home safe or a safety deposit box. If you have a coin collection at home, be careful how you store and handle the coins. Coins are susceptible to dampness. Dropping them will result in damage and a decrease in their worth. Even if you handle them carelessly, it will make a difference. When examining coins, hold them by the edge. Your skin contains a corrosive salt that will tarnish silver coins and harm copper and bronze coins. Coins should not be cleaned in general. The surfaces of the coin will be abraded as a result of cleaning. It has the potential to destroy a desirable patina or luster. Any type of treatment of this nature can more than halve the item's value.

The danger is simply not worth it. This type of therapy is detectable by an expert. Coin collecting is a popular hobby all around the world. There is a market for every taste and interest. This could be the reality whether you are interested in Greek and Roman coins for antiquity's sake, Islamic coins, or coins from the United Kingdom and the United States.

CHAPTER THREE

What is numismatics?

Numismatics, or the study of coins, benefits from a grasp of the historical background of the era and nation you wish to collect from. This might help you to be more delicate and educated in your collection. The following are quick overviews of some of the collectible marketplaces.

What are coin varieties

Coins can be constructed of precious or base metals. They are available in several monetary denominations, exactly as today, and are divided into two major categories: the older hammered version and the more recent milled form.

Coins of Greece and Rome

From an aesthetic viewpoint, these coins are among the most attractive. As the concept moved westward from its beginnings in Asia Minor, Ancient Greece was the first area to be touched by coinage. Many Ancient Greek coins are beautifully crafted.

They frequently feature the patron deities of the city-states that issued them. The coinage of Philip II of Macedon, Alexander the Great's father, traveled throughout the Danube basin. Celtic tribes as far west as Britain adopted them extensively.

If you collect coins like this, keep in mind that rarity, while significant, is less important than condition and beauty. Currently, the market is quite steady. Sicily's Greek coins are regarded as among the most beautiful ever created. The diversity of Roman coinage is virtually limitless and spans seven centuries. They reflect the expansion of Roman civilization from Sudan in the south to Britain in the north, and from Spain in the west to Syria in the east. For over 400 years, Britain was a member of this empire. Coins commemorating Roman Britain, as well as those minted at mints such as London, are extremely collectible.

Ancient coins are a relatively worldwide market, having strong collector and investment bases in Russia, the United States, and Europe, among other places.

Coins of Islam

In practice, this refers to coinage from the Near and Middle East after Islam's emergence in the seventh century. The principles of Islam are reflected on the coins. They do not have any images of people, only Arabic lettering and digits. There are other possibilities.

These contain coins of various Muslim monarchs featuring pictures and inscriptions in languages other than Arabic. Non-Muslim monarchs' coinages, however, follow Islamic norms. Baldwin's carries a large selection of Islamic currency.

Coins of British

The first British coins were primitive, hand-made Celtic offerings. Some were brought over from continental Europe. They circulated in Britain from approximately 150 BC, with locally created issues quickly taking control and lasting until the Roman invasion in 43 AD. These 'Celtic' coins include a wide spectrum of magnificent Celtic artwork, including horses, wolves, wild boar, and a slew of unknown pagan gods.

During this time, mints were functioning in several regions of southern England. Many Celtic tribes minted their own money. They were finally surpassed by Julius Caesar's expeditions and the later Roman invasion of Britain under Claudius in 43 AD. For the next 450 years, official and unofficial Roman currency circulated. It has an excellent range of choices.

This was followed by Anglo-Saxon problems in the tumultuous era that followed the Roman Empire's demise in the West. In this epoch, there are several subdivisions. Among these are coins issued by the Kings of Mercia, Viking coinage, and others. Later, in the late Anglo-Saxon and Norman periods, a more regular succession was formed. By the eleventh century, mintmarks and royal portraits were prevalent on these coins. Coins became more identifiable in this fixed format as time passed. Some centuries later, dates of the issue began to appear on coins.

All of these epochs provide lucrative chances for collecting and investing. However, from the perspective of a collector, the reign of Charles I and the English Civil War are among the most fascinating. This is due to the wide range of coins produced by several mints in areas under Royalist control as the conflict proceeded. There were also the crude pieces hit in cities besieged by Parliamentary forces. Other epochs, on the other hand, are as fascinating. Most reigns have their own set of rarities. Rare occurrences are frequently the outcome of succession changes.

The coins of Edward VIII's brief reign, which began in January 1936 and ended in December of that year, were issued in pattern and proof form. However, they were never widely distributed. There are several examples of how rarities may occur. Edward VIII's coins are exceedingly uncommon, and when they do become available, they may bring tens of thousands of pounds.

For a long time, the value of British coinage has been steadily rising. Over many years, they have provided excellent returns to both collectors and investors. Baldwin experts can provide advice on all areas of collecting British coins from any era.

Coins of the universal

The US coin market has a considerably shorter history of coinage than many other markets. Coin collection is a popular pastime, and coin investment is popular as well. The collection of topics has been mandated by official policy. Previously, the US Mint favored only minor design modifications. There were just 70 distinct circulation currency designs and 60 commemorative issues between 1805 and 1964, for example.

This strategy, however, has been reversed since the mid-1980s. The market has been inundated with problems. Serious collectors are only interested in a few.

This implies that collecting real rarities and mistakes coins minted with an accidental design problem is frequently the focus of numismatics in America. Another collecting theme is to concentrate on a certain set of dates and mintmarks. Because of the richness of the American collector population, rarities in the US fetch many times the price of similar items in the British market. This market is challenging to navigate.

Coins of Continental Europe

In many ways, continental European marketplaces are similar to those of the United Kingdom. However, they have not experienced the same consistent price increases as British coins in recent years.

Collectors in particular European markets tend to focus on coins from their local market. Despite this, a sophisticated network of skilled collectors and dealers exists. European coin collectors are interested in a wide variety of coins from various ages and types. In Europe, ancient coins are extremely popular. It is also critical to avoid overpaying for little goods. This necessitates the use of specialized guidance.

Coins of Russia and China

New affluence in Russia has sparked a boom in interest in Russian art, coinage, and commemorative medals, a hybrid of the two.

Similarly, increased affluence in China as a result of economic reform should lead to an increase in interest in numismatics. However, the Chinese coin industry has always been plagued by significant levels of counterfeiting. As a result, if you want to gather in this region, you must have an expert on standby.

CHAPTER FOUR

How to properly invest in valuable coins?

Coins are a popular form of investment all around the world. The market has been reasonably steady. While not feasible, huge short-term profits in coins are uncommon. Those that keep coins for five to 10 years or more make the most money. As with all collectibles, there are a few ground rules that would-be coin investors must abide by.

The first step is to put aside a certain sum of money for coin investment, either in absolute terms or as a proportion of your investable assets. Many collectors and investors, for example, aim to have 5-10% of their portfolio in physical items such as coins. The coin collecting industry is vast. Serious investors may need to narrow their focus.

So, choose a topic that interests you. Make pick one about which you already have some history or background information if at all feasible. Learn more about it. Speak with a professional who is well-versed in that particular market segment.

Patience is the next essential. Coins in the Slaney collection, as well as those in other recently auctioned collections, such as the Prospero Collection of magnificent ancient gold and silver, obtained their highest returns during 30-50 years. Gaps in your collection may only be filled over time.

How are coins made?

Raw Materials from Mining

The mining of raw materials is the first step in the minting process. Mines in the United States and across the world produce the gold, silver, copper, and other metals necessary. Impurities in the raw metal obtained from these mines make it unsuitable for coinage.

The United States Mint employs recycled metal recovered from different sources in addition to mining ore to acquire the needed metal. Coins that are no longer "machinable" and have been removed from circulation are among these sources. They are then sent to the mint to be recycled into new coins. Refining, melting, and casting are examples of secondary processes.

Almost all impurities are removed from the raw metal during the refining process. Some coins necessitate the use of an alloy of two or more distinct metals. The refined metal is melted, and the extra metals specified are added. The United States Mint, for example, manufactures its five-cent coin from an alloy of 75% copper and 25% nickel.

When the metal has reached the desired purity or alloy, it is cast into an ingot. These are huge metal bars containing the appropriate amount of metal from the mint. Throughout the process, the metal is tested to ensure that the correct purity is attained.

Tossing

Rolling the ingot to the correct thickness may be a time-consuming and tedious operation. The ingot is rolled between two hardened steel rollers that get inexorably closer together. This procedure will be repeated until the ingot is rolled into a metal strip of the correct thickness for the coin being created. Furthermore, the rolling process softens the metal and alters its molecular structure, allowing it to be struck more easily and producing superior quality coins.

Blanking

The US Mint utilizes metal rollers that are roughly 13 inches broad and weigh several thousand pounds. To eliminate the curvature from the production process, the roll of metal is unwound and flattened. It is then sent through a machine that punches out metal discs that are now the correct thickness and diameter for the coin being created.

Polishing

Until now, the manufacturing process for metal blanks has been filthy and run in a hostile atmosphere. Small bits of scrap metal may become mixed up with the coin blanks. The riddling machine removes the correctly sized blanks from any extraneous materials that may have been mixed in with the coin blanks.

Cleaning and annealing

The mint next places the coin blanks in an annealing furnace to soften the metal before striking. The blanks are next immersed in a chemical solution to remove any grease or grime that may have accumulated on the coin's surface. During the striking process, any foreign material that becomes embedded in the coin must be discarded.

Distressing

To preserve the design that will be impressed on the metal coin blank, each coin blank is run through a machine with a series of rollers that grow progressively smaller and impart a raised metal rim on both sides of the coin blank. This procedure also ensures that the coin blank has the correct diameter and will strike correctly in the coining press. The coin blank is now known as a planchet as a result of this procedure.

Striking or stamping

The planchets are now ready for striking after being properly prepped, softened, and cleaned. Business-struck coins are fed into the coining press at a pace of several hundred coins per minute. Proof coins are put into the coining press by hand and receive at least two strikes per coin.

Distribution

Coins that have passed inspection are now ready to be distributed. Business-issued coins are packaged into bulk storage bags and delivered to The Federal Reserve Bank for distribution to local banks. Collector coins are put in specific holders and packaging before being delivered to coin collectors worldwide.

CHAPTER FIVE

Where can to sell valuable coins?

Sell to a Coin Shop

The coin dealer will buy them for less than their true value, which is usual. If the coin store owner paid fair market value for them, he couldn't sell them for a profit. They're operating a company, not a charity, aren't they? So, how much less will the man offer you? A reasonable range would be between 20% and 40% less. Please enable the owner to explain why he is giving what he is offering, and if something smells bad, please leave. It's not a huge deal. Most store owners, on the other hand, are usually fair if you go in expecting to receive somewhat less than the coin's real value. A coin store may be an excellent option if you need to get rid of a large number of coins quickly. Don't be scared to inform the proprietors (politely) that you are shopping the coins around to different stores.

Physical Auction

Look for an auction and inquire if the auction house would be interested in advertising your collection. They will, of course, impose a fee that is either flat or a percentage of the sale price.

Online Auction or Marketplace

This may be the greatest choice in general for people who want to get the most out of their coins and are not constrained by time. Getting your coins sold, one at a go through months, it can be years, is the coolest option to obtain the most profit for your coin collection. But where exactly? We strongly warn against utilizing eBay, or feeBay as it is often known. The costs for listing and selling a coin on eBay are exorbitant.

How to give value to your coin?

Begin by Understanding the Value

If you believe you have a rare coin, do some research on its worth. This will make you a more knowledgeable vendor and prevent you from asking too little for the coin.

Consider a Valuation

A whole coin collection or a particularly costly rare coin may necessitate a professional assessment. Appraisers frequently charge $100 per hour or more, and the entire cost of the assessment as well as the worth of the coin must be considered in your selection. Do you believe the coin or collection is worth a lot of money? If this is the case, the appraisal is well worth it to ensure that you know exactly what you're selling and how much to ask. Appraisals are particularly useful if you want to sell the coin or collection as part of an estate and need to know the legal worth. If you decide to have the coin or collection assessed, make sure you choose a coin appraiser.

Get a feel for your worth

An assessment isn't always a good investment. You might attempt several ways for determining the value of coins that you feel are worth less than the assessment fee:

- Check rare coin price lists in the United States for your coin. If it's there, you've got a place to start.
- Learn about the variables that influence rare coin prices, including scarcity, quality, and demand.
- Search eBay for comparable sold coins. Check only sold ads, as asking prices may not accurately reflect the worth of a coin.
- Check to check if the coin you're interested in is uncommon. Look up the coin's kind, year, and mint.

How to get your coin ready for sale

Before you sell a coin or set of coins, be sure they are in good condition. This entails presenting things elegantly and demonstrating that you are aware of what you have. This will instill trust in purchasers, allowing you to demand top money for the coins.

How to examine the coin holder

Coin holders, also known as slabs, are commonly used to preserve collectible coins from handling. However, much as coins become damaged as they circulate, holders can begin to exhibit substantial wear. Examine the slab to ensure that you can see the coin through it. If it isn't, you should clean it and think about replacing it.

The coins should not be cleaned or polished.

It may be tempting to clean or polish the coins as you prepare to sell them. This should be avoided since it may remove the patina or harm the coin.

Consider getting a CAC sticker

The CAC, or Certified Acceptance Corporation, specializes in grading coins and determining their quality. The CAC will affix a tamper-evident sticker to the coin holder if the coin is in "solid" condition or better. This grading method informs potential purchasers that the coin has been inspected, and it can increase the value of a coin when it is sold. If you believe you have a coin in excellent condition, it may be worth the cost to have it inspected and stamped. Prices range from $15 to $50, depending on the worth of the coin.

How to select the appropriate time to sell coins

Valuable coins will sell at any time, but they may be more valuable to purchasers who are in the market for coins. The trick is to know when to sell your coins. These pointers may be useful:

- Avoid selling at periods when customers may be distracted or distracted, such as holidays, summer vacations, and significant political events such as elections.
- Try to sell when purchasers are likely to have a windfall, such as after-tax season.
- Investigate coin collecting events and sell coins shortly before or after they occur.

How to determine if a collection should be grouped or divided?

If you're selling a coin collection, you should think about splitting it apart. Proof sets should never be divided, although a big collection may be divided in various ways. Many coin collectors do this instinctively, while casual collectors might not. To make a huge collection simpler to sell, it is often necessary to split it into smaller categories. Similarly, numerous individual coins may be put together to encourage sellers. Consider the following groups:

- Prior to 1909, old pennies were minted.
- Buffalo nickels are examples of old nickels.
- Other coins classified by denomination
- Paper money issued by the United States
- Other countries' paper money

United States Rare Coin Prices Guides and Resources

- Best Coin Free Rare Coin Price Guide
- Professional Coin Grading Service
- NumisMedia Fair Market Price Guide

CHAPTER SIX

How to understand the Four Coin Values

When it comes to determining the value of rare United States coins, buying or selling them may be difficult. All antique and collectible goods, including rare coins, have four values.

- The value that the coin's owner believes it is worth.
- The price that the coin's buyer is willing to pay.
- The price is shown in a Price Guide or Red Book.
- The coin's true selling price whether is sold to a private buyer, a dealer, or at an auction.
- Whether you want to purchase or sell rare coins, knowing where to get reliable and timely United States rare coin prices are critical.

Special notes on coin variations

Commemorative coins are issued to commemorate important anniversaries or occurrences. In the past, surcharges were frequently added to the purchase of commemoratives as a method of generating funds for certain causes. Typically, they were silver half dollars, but quarters, dollars, and gold coins were occasionally minted.

With the release of dozens of mainly Half Dollars honoring various events on local, state, and national levels in the 1920s and 1930s, commemorative coins became one of the most popular means of collecting coins in the Twentieth Century. There are two types of commemorative coins issued in the United States: Classics (1892-1954) and Modern releases (1982-present)

Coins from the American colonies

Colonial coins were issued by different governments or private enterprises before the establishment of the United States Mint in 1792. They spread freely across the colonies and, subsequently, the United States. These coins are classified as "Colonial" or Post-Colonial issues. Coins minted before 1783 are referred to as Colonial, while those issued later are referred to as Post-Colonial The bulk of them were copper pieces, which were frequently similar in size and weight to British copper coins of the time.

Gold Coins from the Pioneer Territorial and Early Branch Mints

Pioneer gold coins are appreciated among the most knowledgeable and wealthy collectors. Pioneer gold is also known as Private and Territorial Gold. Between 1830 and 1860, private mints produced the majority of these pieces. Beginning in 1830, Georgia produced some of the first privately minted gold pieces. Gold had been discovered in the state's mountainous areas as well as adjacent Western North Carolina.

Coinage with a Pattern

New designs for our country's coinage are proposed regularly. These new designs are frequently minted as coins and offered to congressional and other committees for approval. Many of the designs are almost identical to others struck at the same time, demonstrating the "tweaking" that was going on to come up with the "just right design" to submit for consideration.

Coins of Today (Including Proofs)

This type of collecting typically refers to coins minted in the United States and across the world after 1964. In the recent decade, modern coins have grown in popularity. Collectors are drawn to them for a variety of reasons, including:

Many groups, like these, Jefferson Nickels, Washington Quarters, Kennedy Half Dollars, Eisenhower Dollars, and Silver Eagles, could be placed in good grade neglecting the six-figure stoppers viewed in many historic issues.

Many collectors strive to get the best grades possible for each date and mintmark in the series they have chosen. When collecting current series, this is a lot simpler aim to achieve.

Beauty: When in mint condition, several of the contemporary coin series are among the most beautiful ever made.

How to recognize a fake coin

Follow your intuition

If a coin seems and feels wrong, whether from the surface or the color, it is most likely counterfeit. Alloys are used in the production of many counterfeit gold coins. These are a different hue than gold coins and appear more like brass. In many cases, these alloy pieces are cast from molds and lack the appropriate surface that a struck coin would have.

Determine the size and weight

You can readily spot a variety of counterfeit coins using a scale and a set of calipers. Many counterfeiters attempt to pass their items off as genuine based on appearance but are unconcerned with specifics. Because alloy counterfeits do not have the same density as gold or silver, their weight will be inaccurate. These can vary from a half gram to a few grams but are not large enough to be related to wear loss. Those attempting to mimic the weight of a real piece will most likely be unable to replicate the diameter and thickness due to the incorrect alloy density.

Pay attention to the intricacies

On rare occasions, a counterfeit coin is manufactured from the same valuable metal as the coin it is attempting to imitate. This is especially true for US gold coins. In this case, we must analyze the specifics of the coin's strike by comparing it to a certified coin. There are occasionally die indications on recognized counterfeits that indicate the actual nature of the coin. There may also be a lack of depth in the design, as well as tiny elements that have been ignored. You can best protect yourself from even the most cunning counterfeits by thoroughly examining the characteristics of coins and consistently handling verified pieces.

CHAPTER SEVEN

How to keep track of your coins?

It is impossible to overstate the significance of categorizing your coin collection. As one seasoned coin collector once put it, "We are only custodians of these little works of art. We will not be able to take them with us when we leave this planet, therefore we must protect them for future generations." If your heirs do not wish to maintain your coin collection, a properly cataloged collection will make it easy for them to liquidate it. Alternatively, you may utilize your coin collection's catalog to select which coins will belong to which heirs of your estate. This method can spare you a lot of hassles and conflicts during the distribution of your estate.

You should give specifics about what's in your collection, how much you paid for it, and possibly how much it's worth now. This will protect your descendants from being taken advantage of when it comes time to sell your coin collection since they will have a notion of its approximate worth.

Furthermore, there are legal ramifications. For tax purposes, the IRS wants documents that substantiate the purchase and sale information for each of your coins. If you or your heirs attempt to sell a coin and do not record the original purchase price or value, the IRS will infer that any money over face value is profit and must be taxed. For tax reasons, any coin received as a gift should be recorded at its current market value. Although this article is not intended to be tax advice, these guidelines will provide you and your heirs with the information they will need in the future regarding your coin collection.

Simple ways to catalog your coins

There are several methods for cataloging your coin collection. Some people choose to keep track of their coin collection transactions on 3x5 cards kept in a cigar box. Others utilize sophisticated computer software to interact with coin collecting databases to value coins. There is no one optimal method for cataloging your collection. You should choose whichever technique gives you the information you want and is comfortable for you to use. The methods listed below are some of the most frequent methods used by people to catalog their coin collections.

Documentation

For a little coin collection, a basic spiral or three-ring notebook would do. You may create columns with a ruler and a pen to enter the information you need to track. You may be as creative as you want and track as much information as you like, but the essential information that should be recorded for every coin is as follows:

- Country Year Mint stamp
- Denomination or kind of variety
- Quantity of Grade (i.e., "50" for a roll of cents)
- Purchase date
- The cost of purchasing
- Date of sale
- Price of sale

Checklist for Purchasing

A coin collecting checklist is another approach to record your coin collection while also planning what coins you want to purchase next. The notebook has freedom of writing and beginning information is low, checklists are structured for each series of US coins via the following type, denomination, year, and mint mark.

Spreadsheet

If you have a computer and a simple spreadsheet application (such as Microsoft Excel), you can use it to keep track of your coin collection as well as all of your buy and selling information. This allows you to easily add and delete lines, organize your collection, and immediately determine the total worth of your coin collection. Furthermore, you may opt to track information that other people are not interested in tracking. Simply add a column to your spreadsheet to do this.

You may make tabs for each of your coin folders, albums, collections, and so on. Put name on each tab for it to carry a similar title to your collection. This makes it easy for your heirs to match up your currency album with the spreadsheet that explains what's within.

You may keep track of crucial information for identifying and classifying your collection within each tab. Such data should fall into the same categories as those described above.

To keep track of the overall worth of your collection for that sheet, put running totals to the top or bottom of each column. We recommend placing the totals at the top of the columns so that when you add things to your collection towards the bottom of the spreadsheet, you don't overwrite the totals functions in that cell.

Software

The fourth and best alternative is to buy software designed specifically for coin collectors. There are several coin cataloging software solutions available on the market today. Others are free, some are extremely low-cost ($20-$30), and some are slightly pricier.

What to look for in coin cataloging software: simplicity of use, logically set out panels, the flexibility to arrange your collections as you wish, download current pricing information, and automatically re-value your coin collection at market rates. Finally, and most importantly, search for a fully functional trial version or a money-back guarantee if you are dissatisfied with your purchase.

According to the collectors we've spoken with over the years, there are three main providers of coin collecting software:

- Collector's Assistant by Carlisle Development
- Exact Change by Wild Man Software
- Coin Elite by Trove Software

How to sort coins

The fundamental goal of coin grading is to assess the coin's market worth. The worth of a coin is determined by how effectively the coin was struck initially, the coin's degree of preservation, and the amount of wear and damage it has experienced. Accepting the reality, especially for beginners, the focus would be on how to examine the degree of wear on the coin and where it doesn't meet the 70-point scale.

How to use the Coin Grading Scale of 70 Points?

Numismatists assign coins a numerical value on the Sheldon Scale when they grade them. The Sheldon Scale has grades ranging from Poor (P-1) to Perfect Mint State (MS-70).

Originally, coins were evaluated by employing adjectives to indicate their state (Good, Fair, Excellent, Etc.). Unfortunately, coin collectors and dealers had varying interpretations of what each of these phrases signified.

In the 1970s, professional numismatists came together and established Coin Grading standards. These numismatists now issue grades at critical places on this seventy-point scale, with the most often utilized numeric points being used in conjunction with the original adjective grade. The following are the most frequent coin grades:

(P-1) Poor

Indistinguishable and potentially damaged; must have a date and mintmark if used, otherwise rather battered.

(FR-2) Fair

Nearly smooth, but without the damage that a coin graded Poor generally possesses. Enough information must remain to identify the currency

(G-4) Good

Heavily worn, with lettering blending into the rims in spots and key features mostly destroyed.

(VG-8) Quite Good

The item is very weathered, but all key design features are visible, albeit faintly. There is little if any, core detail left.

(F-12) Fine

Very worn, but even wear, and the overall design features show out strongly. Rims are almost completely isolated from the field.

(VF-20) Very Fine

Moderately weathered, but some finer features remain. All letters of the word LIBERTY and the motto are legible. Both sides of the coin have complete rims that are separated from the field.

(EF-40) Extremely Fine

Very light wear; all devices are clear, and significant devices are bold. Finer detail is strong and visible but may show signs of mild wear.

(AU-50) Uncirculated

Slight indications of wear on high areas of the coin's design; contact marks may exist; eye appeal should be satisfactory.

(AU-58) Extensive Selection Uncirculated

Slight indications of wear, no substantial contact marks, nearly complete mint brilliance, and great eye appeal.

(MS-60) Mint State Basal

Strictly uncirculated; no wear on the highest points of the coin, but an unattractive piece with muted shine, visible contact marks, hairlines, and so on.

(MS-63) Mint State Acceptable

Uncirculated, but with contact marks and nicks, a slightly diminished shine, and an overall attractive look. The strike is of mediocre to poor quality.

(MS-65)

Uncirculated with great mint shine, very little contact marks, and superb eye appeal. The strike rate is higher than normal.

(MS-68)

Uncirculated with excellent shine, no obvious contact marks to the naked eye, and outstanding eye appeal. The strike is both sharp and appealing.

(MS-69) Mint State Almost Superb

Uncirculated with perfect brilliance, a crisp and appealing strike, and extremely good eye appeal. Except for minor imperfections in the planchet, striking, or contact markings (seen only at 8x magnification), this coin is flawless.

Mint State Perfect (MS-70)

The ideal coin. Under 8x magnification, there are no tiny defects evident; the strike is crisp, and the coin is precisely centered on a flawless planchet. Bright and full, with original shine and eye appeal is rarely seen on a coin.

CHAPTER EIGHT

How to use the Three Grade Buckets for Sorting Coins?

From the perspective of a newcomer, the most misunderstood aspect of coin grading is how the grading scale works. Consider it as having three "buckets."

The first bucket contains circulated coins, the second contains approximately uncirculated (AU) coins, and the third contains uncirculated (Mint State, or MS) coins.

Circulated coins have the broadest grading scale. These grades range from P-1 to EF-49. P-run, or poor, is the lowest possible grade for a coin. Even though it has heavy wear and most of the detail has been worn away, this coin is barely recognizable. At the high end of the scale, this would be a circulated coin with minor wear on the coin's highest points. This keeps it from falling into the About Uncirculated category.

Similarly, the AU portion of the scale begins at 50 and continues to 59. The AU-50 coin may never have circulated in commerce, but it is no longer in Mint State because it has scuff marks, has been through several coin-counting machines, and has been handled a small amount.

So, we put it in the AU bucket and assign it an AU-50 if it's ugly and an AU-58 if it's not. This is an oversimplification, but it explains why the grading scale appears to go from "appealing coins" to "ugly coins" and back to "appealing coins."

The MS scale (from MS-60 to MS-70) is not simply a continuation of the previous AU coin scale. It is a completely different mini-scale of 11 grades, beginning with the "base condition" MS-60 Uncirculated coin. This is a drab, bag-marked dog, yet it is officially Uncirculated. In comparison, the AU-58-coin underneath it has a pleasing appearance and virtually full shine. A coin that has an AU-58 grade appears significantly finer than a coin that receives an MS-60 rating. Furthermore, they are indifferent "buckets" of the grading scale.

What is the best way to grade Circulated Coins?

The third bucket contains circulated grades ranging from P-1 to EF-49 (though EF-45 is the most likely circulated grade you'll see being utilized). Most novices seeking grading assistance have circulating coins, which are luckily the easiest for the novice to grade. It's helpful to have a Mint State (a.k.a. uncirculated) specimen of the coin type in question to compare it to, but it's not required.

Step one

First and foremost, you'll need a good light source, such as a 100-watt bulb in a lamp near where you're seated. Note, one needs efficient magnification, obtain one that can magnify 5 to 8 times. Anything more than 8x is rarely used in coin grading, while anything less than 5x is too weak to discern critical features and minor damage signs.

Step two

Decide which "bucket" your currency belongs in. Is it uncirculated (in mint condition)? Is there simply minor wear on the high points (about Uncirculated)? Or does it fit into the most prevalent category, Circulated coin?

Step three

Examine your coin to the scale seen above to see where it falls on the scale. Remember that the figures are not proportionate; in other words, the amount of detail loss between EF-40 and EF-20 is not the same as the amount of detail loss between MS-60 and EF-40 (remember, they're in separate buckets). In actuality, the coin graded EF-40 has lost only around 5% to 10% of its detail, but the coin graded F-20 has lost nearly 60%. Use the provided descriptions to put your coin as accurately as possible. If you desire more accurate grading,

Pictorial Coinage of The United States

Half Cents

Liberty Cap Left   Liberty Cap Right   Draped Bust
1793   1794-1797   1800-1808

Classic Head   Braided Hair
1809-1836   1840-1857

Large Cents

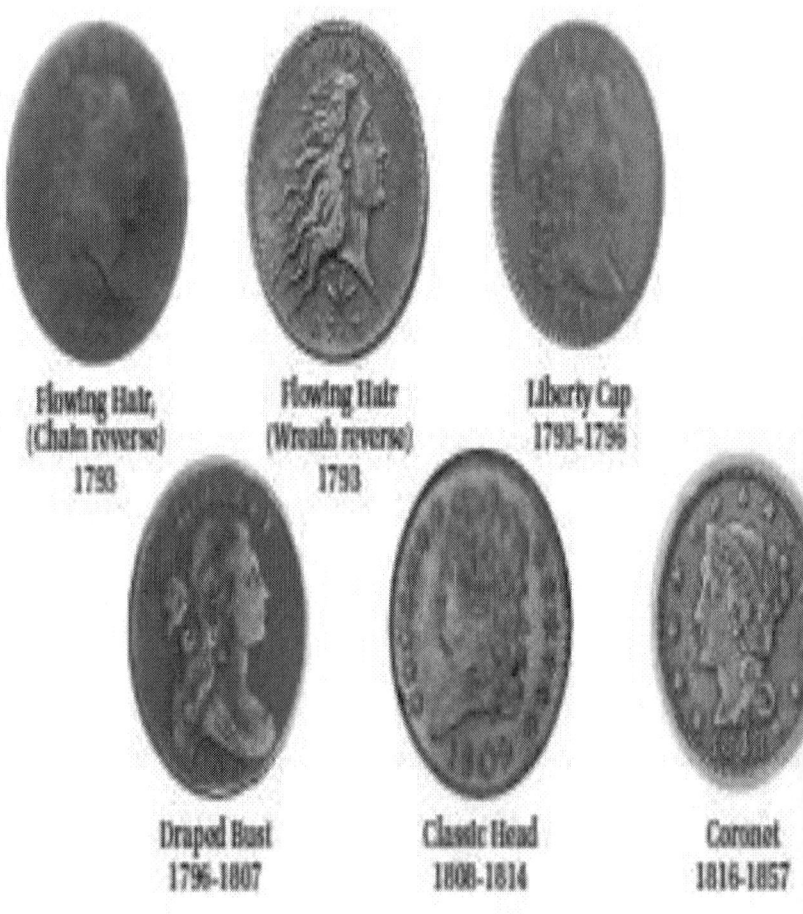

Flowing Hair, (Chain reverse) 1793

Flowing Hair (Wreath reverse) 1793

Liberty Cap 1793-1796

Draped Bust 1796-1807

Classic Head 1808-1814

Coronet 1816-1857

Small Cents

Wheat Ears Reverse   Memorial Reverse
1909-1958   1959-2008

Presidency   Union Shield
2009 Reverse   2010-date

Two Cents Pieces

Three Cents

Half Dimes

Flowing Hair 1794-1795   Draped Bust 1796-1805

Capped Bust
1829-1837

Liberty Seated
1837-1873

Nickels

Twenty Cents

Twenty-Cent Piece
1875-1878

Quarter Dollars

Draped Bust
1796-1807

Capped Bust
1815-1838

Liberty Seated
1838-1891

Barber
1892-1916

Standing Liberty
1916-1930

Washington
1932-1998

Half Dollars

One Dollar

Gold Coins

Made in the USA
Coppell, TX
07 December 2021